Anthony R. Mc Collin is a poet, educator and motivational speaker from the Caribbean twin island, State of Trinidad and Tobago. Born in 1990, he grew up in Clifton Hill, in the Capital City of Trinidad. He is the holder of a Bachelor of Science Degree in Social Studies (Andrews University), a Masters of Science Degree in Government (University of the West Indies) and a Diploma in Management (UWI School of Business & Applied Studies). Despite being a closet writer for most of his life, Anthony believes that poetry is an excellent medium to address critical issues through focusing on topics such as social inequity, hatred, crimes, corruption, gender, sexuality, poverty, religious intolerance, politics, youth and relationships. His approach to writing incorporates the common practice in the Caribbean of storytelling and seeks to reach the hearts, minds and consciences of readers, in order to bring about greater awareness, responsiveness and inclusivity.

Linda Frank,

You were the first 'Jane Doe' I encountered and loved. I admired your strength, simplicity and peaceful spirit. I thank God for allowing me the privilege of being your son. Your children miss you daily.

Rest in sweet peace until we share paradise together!

Anthony R. Mc Collin

Being Jane Doe

The Mind of a Woman Through the Hands of a Man

Austin Macauley Publishers™

LONDON · CAMBRIDGE · NEW YORK · SHARJAH

Copyright © Anthony R. Mc Collin 2021

The right of Anthony R. Mc Collin to be identified as author of this work has been asserted by the author in accordance with section 77 and 78 of the Copyright, Designs and Patents Act 1988.

All rights reserved. No part of this publication may be reproduced, stored in a retrieval system, or transmitted in any form or by any means, electronic, mechanical, photocopying, recording, or otherwise, without the prior permission of the publishers.

Any person who commits any unauthorized act in relation to this publication may be liable to criminal prosecution and civil claims for damages.

A CIP catalogue record for this title is available from the British Library.

ISBN 9781528988711 (Paperback)
ISBN 9781528988728 (ePub e-book)

www.austinmacauley.com

First Published 2021
Austin Macauley Publishers Ltd®
1 Canada Square
Canary Wharf
London
E14 5AA

I want to thank God for the inspiration and His divine presence through the journey of writing this book. Thanks to all the women who came forward and bravely told their stories and shared parts of themselves with me. Your strength and courage is indeed admirable.

Introduction

Being Jane Doe is a collection of poems written to capture the life experiences, ideas and journeys of women at difference stages in their lives, through a series of interviews and conversations. This diverse group of women made themselves accessible and shared their personal and professional high and low experiences with the aim of their stories reaching millions of people through the art of poetry. Those experiences are now transformed into a living body of work that can be used as a testimony of the strength of women.

This poetry collection is a reflection of the common nature of womanhood; it solidifies the idea that women share much more in common than what sets them apart. The themes which emerged through preparing this collection include; love, sexuality and relationships, self-harm and surviving abuse, parental relationships and family life, pregnancy and motherhood, religion and spirituality and self-worth and identity.

Women and men are invited to submerge themselves into this body of literate as it highlights our own struggles, joys and experiences, while also echoing the sentiment that we are not in this world alone. Our independent journey as human beings can be used to inspire and enhance the lives of those around us.

The experience of every Jane Doe, especially the women and young girls who revealed their own "Jane Doe" experiences for the purpose of making this publication a reality, is a reminder to all that there is a Jane Doe living inside every woman; her story deserves to be told and her story deserves to be read.

Theme: Self-Worth and Identity

Self-Discovery

Imagine being the woman with all the strength
of this world resting comfortable around your hips,
And as you stand in the mirror, you
notice how much beauty exist on the
perfect shape of your lips. Those lips
pronounce excellence in every form
and they birth radical thinking for a long-awaited
revolutionary storm.
Imagine being the girl that is never too
weak or too shy.
Can you see yourself as the woman
breaking glass ceilings and floating
effortlessly through the sky?
Let's soul search and live boldly and
with pride. Let's open our conscience
and reveal our hearts to the world.
Jane Doe is on a journey of self
discovery and her home is in every
woman and girl.

The Smell of Victory

My love, do you know the smell of the colour victory?

If not, let me share it with thee.
It tastes like the vibrant motion of swaying
trees that were lost in stagnation, but finally
grew the branches that would dance to the
perfect breeze.
It is the shade of confidence that now glows in
the brightest light,
It glows because light is dark when my light shines this bright!
It smells like the taste of self-worth, which
comes bouncing off my taste buds; too hot to
stay in my mouth, so at every chance I sing
and I shout: freedom! Freedom!
Freedom is the colour of victory and it smells
like the gentle ocean that knows no boundary!
Yes! This new me has the texture of the
sweetest rose that knows where to plant itself
and chooses carefully the hands that will pick
her petals. And chooses carefully the nose that
will be enchanted by her scent,
And that is the smell of the colour victory.

A fragrance that has conquered this world to
live at war with a vicious enemy,
The smell of the colour victory is the survivor
of violence seated perfect and pretty,
In this dark and lonely alley,
Seated alone to smell the colour of her soon-to-be victory.

Some Girls

Some girls dream of white dresses,
and fancy houses fenced by a perfect man;
While some girls dream forever to be
the wife that every husband wants.

Then some girls don't care too much
about love and wedding bells,
Instead life happens as it happens,
and she becomes content with
'all's well that ends well.'

So when motherhood and love
dawned my pretty sky,
I trusted the perfect timing
set strictly between God and I.

Yes, if you look at me now,
You'll feel the glow of feet planted
firmly on the earth,
With a head held high to the sky,
now that I'm giving life to the story
of motherhood as a charming bride.

I've been to the battle room of delivery
all but twice, but I lost soldiers at war
just as many times and mastered the art
of giving myself away so that
others might experience life.

Some girls don't live to share the story,
But I survived every kiss of death
sent forward to seduce me.

Can't you see the magic in these feet
as they dance away from
every wicked tongue with jealous eyes?

And yes, these feet trample the voices
that gossip indiscriminately about being
a better mother that I could ever be.

Imagine the blatant hypocrisy!
Imagine sweet kisses from family!

But swords are no match for a gunslinger,
So your words will find no place in my chest
and your tongue will wave the white flag
to surrender on the sweet sweet day
that you live to see me be
nothing like you mother.

Just imagine,
sweet kisses from family
but their hearts can't wish the best for me.

Some girls don't grow like their mother,
So understand that I am not just a woman
but a strong independent warrior
who fought miscarriage after miscarriage,
but never lost her heavenly armour,
So my voice still tells a story
though these scars trace deeply
through my psyche.

Yes,
some girls dream, search and find
while others live and die

and then,
some girls are like me.

Meeting Jane Doe

When I met Jane, she was the most
careful girl I knew.
Her hair was always its natural colour
and she never forgot to say please
and thank you.

But as time eased its way through us,
I saw a side of her that left me anxious;

Jane was wild and carefree,
She was bold and chatty.
Her eyes were deep and piercing,
But her soul was never anything
less than a home for those
seeking acceptance.

I Am That Woman

Have you ever forgotten what it means
to be free or dance to the beat
of your own drums and sing out of tune
to the enchanting melody of selfishness.

Yes, as a woman I've dance before
while singing countless years of freedom,
But now I've surrendered open fields
For the selfless journey of being a mother,
For the selfless journey of being his wife,
For the selfless, selfless journey of being
somebody that I used to know.

To become the woman that nobody
seems to know.

The woman who needs to be reminded
it's alright to rise at night and cry,
Or to feel the world on her shoulders
while the burden grows heavy
and every hope for peace falls
gingerly from the sky.

I'm that woman seated listening
intently to your fears while my heart races
at the thought of dwindling years.

I'm that lady seated next to you in church
questioning the meaning of life,
Or the feeble nature of all things
planted here on earth.

I'm the girl sitting staring resentfully
at her mother while biting my nails
as I dream of being good enough for her.

I am the wife with a husband
made of pure white stone;
His heart is sweet and his intentions noble,
But his shell seems impenetrable
by fear, anger or worry.
This man is the male version of what
my mind hopes it could be.

So while I have forgotten how to dance
to the drums of freedom,
And my feet are tired and battered,
My heart is at ease when I see myself
glow in the mirror.

I am every woman I've ever met
and I am still a mother.

Getting It Off My Chest

If I had to write some words to my
pretty younger self, I'd say that
I still yearn for a sense of belonging
and for the gentle touch of acceptance
to cuddle my insecurities into remission,
But I had to grow used to cloudy skies
traversed by black birds howling loudly
as they speed past every dream
I had of a happy home
painted with white walls and golden tiles.

Give me a pen and paper and ask
for a note to my siblings,
I'd probably never stop writing
or issue a strong rebuke and firm warning,
Ensuring that they know I'm still standing,
waiting, patiently waiting, for peace
to come rushing through this door,
And for peace to usher in the silence
we need to put this crowded house in order.

And if I had to write a letter to my mother,
I'd ask her how perfection tastes,
Since I've never had it on my tongue
because she managed to arrogantly
consume every drop for all of humanity.

Oh, and if I had to pen a few words
to my husband, I'd ask him to open up
and let me see where his emotions sleep,
Or to dance with me under the stars
while singing eternally, "Every thing
will be okay, yes baby, it will be okay."

But of all my letters,
the letter to me
is certainly the greatest and longest of all
because while the words are few,
the depth and substance are immortal.
In the most generous and gentle way
I'd write 'brave'.

The Artist's Dilemma

How do I colour this canvas,
With broken hands and a busy heart?
These shades will all seem dull,
Standing in the midst of this world's
Bright and more creative light.

So today I'll sit trusting in an inspiration,
From tomorrow's greatest trials,
Because a gift to an artist
is hell, heartache and lies.

What can I paint when the skies
always seem blue? Or when
birds chirp sure of receiving their just due?

There must be some damaged part of me
That can give way to a masterpiece!
But where do I go to rebuild,
After I destroy myself searching
For this deadly truth on a paint brush?

So tonight, I'll rest early and hang up
these dry brushes, ever thirsting for colour.

I'll sit satisfied with my portion,
Full and comforted by every shadow in this empty house.

But tomorrow I must begin the day,
Hopeful to awake this sheet with colour,
Or anything worthy of recognition.

Tomorrow I will hope for darkness:
Some trouble,
Some inspiration.

Take My Advice

Young girl, I see you standing there,
Waiting on the permission of this world;
Be bold and give yourself the care that it
deserves and needs to live.

Drop your guard and become a prisoner
of happiness; this place will never tell
you sorry, so live in it
with a pinch of sassiness.

Give this space the fresh breath that is
your sense of style, and watch the people
become infected with truth, even if for a
short, temporary time.
Watch these people live and breathe and
rise against every angry tide.

Your energy flows from the heart of
your womb, and you are blessed; you are
designed for the universe to see and
embrace and consume.

My love, trust the love in your heart,
Trust, that it's with you, that love,
deserves to start.

My only dream for you is that you be
bold in this cold and selfish world,
My only dream for you is that in this
world, they discover that you are bold!

Just wait, your story is still waiting to be told.
My only dream for you, young girl,
is that you become bold!

Stranger in My Skin

I feel like a stranger while living in my
own skin, I've constantly battled the
enemy that lives deep within.

Dark nights and stormy days are all that
hound over my town, because the sun
refuses to shine and I have very little time
to think of any good reason why I
deserve any bright light in my life.

I have heard every insult that a teen girl
needs to hear; now when I watch in the
mirror, I don't expect anything beyond a
blank and awkward stare.
A gaze maybe,
Or a pensive look into a soul waiting on
the beautiful girl's story to finally be told.

What story does she even have?
It starts with once upon a time and
ends with a dramatic scene,

Where she runs away from the haunted
town and drowns herself in a stream of tears.

Welcome to Womanhood

Does every woman feel what I feel,
Or am I the only one that wishes
she could vanish into thin air,
Just to escape the rude comments,
And unjustified awkward stares.

Does he know I'm filthy and unclean,
Or is he thinking of why women act
moody and obscene all for a few days,
All for a few days,
then we are back to being the world's
greatest gift and the perfect sex machine.

Oh, and look at this awful sight!
Does she know there is a stain on her rear?
I hope a boy doesn't see it so I better rush
over there, "Excuse me sister, please stop so
I can help you hide this curse,"
Is the usual line of a heroine as she reaches
down into her well-stocked purse.

And this is our journey,
Month after month
Year after year,
Standing in a corner draped in self-pity
and confused with by a platter of emotions,
Jogging senselessly through our hearts
And minds concurrently,
Just like a poverty-stricken mother
with a wealth of patience but little time,
So we keep our eyes open for every washroom
and the nearest wall
to hide our shame for a moment
while checking our body for leaks
and whisper a sigh.

Ah, yes but a woman's work is never over,
So the only time this blessing might cease,
is as we welcome for nine months,
the task of being a carrier and host for another.

Hello, sister!
Were you ever prepared for this
monthly act of labour?

No, no! Never!

Someone should have warned you
that your life changes forever.
Or advised you that even during this time,
You're still worthy of respect and love,
Just like any other.

And here she comes again,
Rushing through my system,
Like waves in ocean hurry to touch the shoreline,
And here I am again,
Fully conscious of what this means,
And completely learning
the rise and fall of womanhood.

No Ordinary Human

If you want ordinary, then leave me alone
because I've never had dreams of domestication
or colouring within the lines.

And I don't play by the rules,
My hands are caked over
with untamed ambition so I have
no use for you or time to lose.

Pink dresses or flowers on Valentine's
don't make my eyes or underwear wet,
So you should step back for a moment
while I ease my way from the shadow
of men drowning in regret.

Regret for not valuing the shade's beauty,

Regret for failing to measure the strength
of my heart correctly.

Regret for his awkward and silly gaze
as he looks at me packing; eagerly ready
to turn this page.

I'm no ordinary human,
I've danced around rapist and slayed
wealthy dragons,
So if a working woman who doesn't sit
with her stomach neatly tucked in
is a threat, then write your will and prepare
for your immediate death.

Ladies do this and ladies do that!
I'm not a "lady" I'm a human being
who deserves every drop of respect,
So I won't paint my nails or stand in heels
just to satisfy your ego while preparing
your favourite meals.

So if you're looking for places to kiss
because of the perfection you want,
I'll leave you to choose.
The rear,
Or the front.

Dancing on My Grave

Mourning and weeping should fill the night's
sky, but watch me now, dancing and singing
As I bury this life I once tried to hide.

Follow the pattern of my feet moving
smoothly over this grave, leaving no stone
unturned; stamping the dirt flat with the dregs
of my bottled-up rage.

Don't bring any tears of mourning to this
funeral parlour! I'm far too excited to erase
skeletons that if left unchecked, could turn this
world over and over and over.

Feel the tempo of the music as I dance with
style and grace! My light heart and bright
smile could make a mockery of this dark
and gloomy place,
But let me dance to the tune of life, as I've
made it out alive through grace and grace
and grace.

Death, to the insecurities that plagued
my youth!
Death, to a fear of not being good enough
for you!
Death, to the pain I felt inside, each time I saw
a mother and daughter standing with pride!
Death to addiction and self-inflected war!

Death to a life I've come to abhor.

Watch me dancing so passionately over
this grave,
I will not mourn the past,
Because I was worth being saved!

I Am That Woman

I am that woman you should fear, but not
because of my rage or the way I stare.

You should fear my intelligence because it
defeats every structure you've place in this
world to keep me back.
Fear my hands because unlike my heart,
They are soft and far from cold,
I am the woman that runs this world.

I am that woman you should fear;
Don't expect me to stand aside and cry,
The power of my work destroys every lie
that shouts, 'Women can't get by.'

I am the woman driving perfectly with
confidence, as you arrogantly wait for me to
cause the next road accident and grunt,
'It must be a woman.'

I am the woman you should fear, since with
me this place will never be the same;

Your markets will crumble, and poverty will
no longer be a part of a nasty political game!

I am that woman you should fear,
Because I am the woman who knows herself.
So little man,
Beware!

Being a Little Girl

Little girls are to be seen but not heard,
So I shot my mouth each time
my bedroom door was cracked,
But an uninvited demon,
Ravaging through my youth,
And destroying my worth.

Big girls don't cry,
So I bottled all this rage deep inside,
Hoping that one day God would come,
And accept me despite my weirdness,
Or inability to love anyone.

Women must know their place,
So I stood in the corner waiting to die.
I kept my ideas as secrets,
And I never learnt how to fly.
So my friend, glass ceilings are a mockery
because there is nothing worth
reaching for over me.

Little girls must be seen but not heard,
So here I am in my second childhood,
Suffering at every moment,
Battling every teardrop,
And waiting for the sun to set
on my face.

Little girls must be seen but not heard,
Until we are all gone and they all realise
that we're the reason they lived,
To tell us to be quiet.

Mirror Talk

Who is this woman that dares to look me in my eyes?
Why does she reach out to me with equal desire
when I stretch to offer some help?
Such a poor, poor soul.

I'm not standing here trying to be your sister,
Nor identify with the struggles you wear,
Or that bruised your shoulder.
I am here because
pity directed me to your awful shoreline
on the ocean of emptiness and tragic
faith in the beauty of this world.

Stand back! Don't you come too close to me!
Your skin glows in the colour of deceit,
While your teeth form the cage for a tongue
that beats lies through the streets.

Stand back! I don't trust those bright green eyes.
They remind me of a forest filled with fruits
of envy. Oh, and how much you love to love,
And love with envy.

So it hurts each time I walk past the windows
of shops in this town. The merchants all scream
at what they call an unshakable resemblance.

I squirm to think that I could one day look
like you, and I'd die the most gruesome of deaths
if what this mirror says is proven to be true.

The Wild Flower

Jane Doe is the wild flower
designed with a unique DNA
that allows her to grow
and bloom,
In any place,
At any time,
Against all odds.

Jane is a wild flower
designed with the perfect DNA.

Hello, Jane!

The New Me

I keep finding parts of myself
in people and things that barely even know.
It's like meeting someone new each day,
Or every moment that I face the demons
and grow.

My beauty is made up of so many elements now;
I'm bigger than my skin and perfectly shaped
eyebrows. My smile actually means I'm happy,
And the shadows of my past no longer
have the same effect of stealing my glow.

I've discovered some truth about love and lust,
And how one affects the other, and neither is
worth a second without trust.
But the fancy things of this world still fail
to bring me joy. There is little difficulty in me
accepting I'm one of this world's simple
little girls.

Imagine me, perfectly fine standing
in my nakedness. I refuse to cover my skin with

lies, or hide the beauty of my heart which sits
curiously on my chest and elevated by my
perky new breasts.

And finally, this caged bird is free,
Living the life of a lion, hunting for
prey which once hunted me.

I keep finding parts of myself
in people and things I never knew.
I'm going to places far and wide,
And dancing on fresh green grass
in places familiar too.

Theme: Love, Sexuality and Relationships

Love Triangle

Love, lust and learning are all little parts of me,
Twisted into the perfect triangle,
And glued together by curiosity.

My heart, my mind and body,
All have a brain of their own.
And with you I've lost control;
They are now yours to own.

Three languages confuse my presence,
Time after time it encounters you,
But here I am,
Ready to let my body have you,
But my mind attacks jealously,
And my heart speaks in a tongue
of pleasure or possession.

If I were to have my way,
Hesitantly, I'd whisper that
You should only be mine,
But these fluent conversations
confuse every part of my core

because since I've known myself,
I've been the only thing I wanted,
Until now.

But maybe, this chaotic
assembly of thoughts
keep my spirit awake
with a thirst for you,
because our love is matched
like the gender identity
we commonly pursue.

The One Noah Left Behind

How dare you tell me this is an evil spirit
when all I feel is a reality of love.

This world with all its protocol
has ruined every chance
I have for true and unconditional love.

My heart beats twice as fast when I see her,
And like Romeo and Juliet, this is to the end.
Her kisses still confuse every part of
my carefully shaped body,
As though we were married to last forever,
And the light that shines through
the dark decision, reveals a promise
of paradise and eternal life.

Even though the constructs
of this bigoted world tell us no,
Can't we stand before priest or judge
and pledged to the end?
If this doesn't last,
I'll know I ran this race too late,

So I'll regret my pretence
for survival behind my youthful prison gates.

Biological or not, I want to be a mother,
Not my mother though,
Since I will give birth
to every good thing
your innocent pure heart can desire.
The only difference here,
Is that we are the ones who feel
This forbidden magic
riding on steroids of lust
To the garden of love,
And while they have shot us out
like the animals their God asked Noah
to leave behind,
We will blossom in my heart
And I'll sit patiently waiting
For your love story built in a house of denial
To end, so that ours can begin,
secretly.

Jane Doe – Trapped in the Closet

I've been hiding in this dark place since
I came to know myself,
I'm afraid to come out because the world
is waiting for me.

What if they chase me with torture
stakes, or burn me upside down on a
cross for their own awkward satisfaction.

There is no room in the tightly packed
streets for a woman dressed like me.
In fact, there is no room in the streets for
anyone other than those that resemble
the law.

So I'm wrapped between these clean
sweaters and trapped in dirty underwear,
Waiting for some stranger to validate my
existence with a ruling from the highest court.

But on Judgement Day,
They will have to remove my lifeless

body from among these freshly washed linens,
Because I'd rather die in the closet than come out and be told I'm allowed to live with normal folks.

Wet Dreams

Jane, my friend,
At night,
You find yourself
Immersed and wet
Reaching for
The dry washcloth,
Confused and hurry
to wipe each memory
that reaches this far
down your sheet.

Only to discover
The reason you cry
Is your reason to change
this bed linen.

What confusing pleasure
When your pillow is dry now,
But you're turning in puddles.

Beauty and the Beast

I love fairy-tales with happy endings and
sweet love songs. Things like that make
simple hearts of city girls into anything but an
oxymoron.

I like pretty dresses with well-done hair and
make-up that fit perfectly over the scars you
clawed into my quickly forgiving soul.

And, oh how I dreamt for years of having my
love rush through town, eager to find my feet,
or fingers to slide on them a shoe or wedding
ring; making me the perfect princess to a
handsome prince.

But when you came, you brought the shame of
toxic masculinity covered with a filthy shade
of manipulation that made me stay and stay
and stay and stay.

Trusting that each bruise would ago away and
every drop of blood poured from my cup

would be the thirst quencher that finally ended
this horror and press play to the start of a fairy-tale;
Beauty and the Beast, happily ever after.

The Self-Struggle and Divorce

Standing at this gateway I can tell we
both want and deserve different things,
But it's hard to verbalise when life is
tied up with conventions and
demands about each and every thing.

You deserve a love that is carefree
and boundless, but I want a husband
that will just hold me close to his chest.

You are fighting with truth and hurt
and pounds of insecurities, but I want
a house and life fortified with armed
security and the best technology.

The tears you cry come from deep
within your stomach. They tell stories
of unresolved trauma and of a girl
who was left unchecked. But my tears
never flow in a public space. I have
work to do and I refuse to be any
man's dead weight.

You want to explore the world, climb
mountains and swim across the ocean
while I have no interest in taking a
risk regardless of how wide my
wounds spread open.

You deserve to go but I want to stay
as this marriage gets crowded day after
day after day.

I hate mirrors because they create a
dialogue we might not be ready to
have, so instead of facing my enemies,
I'll run past them and watch my soul
and body starve.
There will be no fresh air and self-
care in this place.
Pull yourself together because marriage
is the only way!

The Marriage Act

My husband finishes what God started in me,
And I really believe this is what marriage is
meant to be.

The awkward stares don't intimidate my view
because I've wrapped myself in an
unsurmountable confidence,
A confidence dressed in white,
A confidence of a forever bride,
The confidence of a never-ending wedding ring
engraved with His love,
Polished by our truth.

God finishes what my husband begins
each day in me;
A whisper that our journey is one that
requires a partner,
A dream kissed gently to the forehead; a kiss
that drives a sharp sword through my enemy of
self-doubt.

Who would ever believe that a kiss could kill their enemy?

Love and War

When the dust settles,
Every soldier sent forward
Will return to their bases,
Bruised and belittled,
Tired, dragging the dead horses
we sent them galloping forward on.

This war was never meant
to enter history books or be etched on paper,
Or record our sweet confusing chemistry,
But here we stand dripping white blood
and fighting to tie red bandages
around open wounds and scared egos.

Oh, sweet love of mine,
Are you confused by the purity and innocence
which leaks through our awful wounds?
Or are you surprised by the passion of
forgiveness and zeal to nurse each other
back to perfect health?

There is only smoke in this place now,
'cause the dust has collected at our feet,
And every flame has died a shameful death.

But where there is smoke the heat is still sure,
And where there is heat, a speck of a flame
lies waiting to be gassed, fed and harnessed
into a blaze that once was.

This is our time now to burn the envious tongue;
This is our time to be refined and reborn;
This is our time to live and spread
a flame to those who will never know
what it means to love.

Until this smoke gives way.

For Better and for Worse

Sometimes my husband doesn't hear
me, but I've come to learn that can be
the worse of him,
At times when my husband listens to
me, he brings the world to a stop and
life is worth living again.

Love is meant to be trusted even
when it seems so unstable
because the one we are loving isn't
made of bolts and knots or cables.

Just imagine for a moment what this
world would be like if no one ever
found true love or decided to risk it
all while plunging head-first into this
dark tunnel without a light in sight.

And sometimes, just sometimes, if we
are honest and true, we might reveal
our full self to the other and that can
get ugly and messy too!

Demons rage and uncleaned wounds
might erupt with puss but in that
moment, we get to test our faith
and destiny since there is no easy way
in 'together forever'.

I've heard stories of this romance and
how love might be a curse,
But I'll write my own narrative and
we will be the characters;
For better and for worse.

Learning Love Languages

I've learnt that every human being
speaks a different language while hoping
the translations share a common meaning.

Love is said in many ways:
Sometimes, its truest form is in a simple
and gentle gaze of your lover,
And,
The helpful hand of a father
who never fails to provide clothing,
food and shelter.

Or it can be found deep in the eyes of a
mother; a woman who finds courage to
reveal her mistakes and the strength to
guide you away from them.

Love can be translated from a language
that is ugly and abusive;
because hidden below his anger
is corrupt childhood so I discovered
that his language was distorted.

Reaching in Deep

If I pull you inside of me
There is no limit to the places we'd go.
We'd be constantly surfing desires
to keep you happy,
And to see you glow.

Kissing you releases a toxin
I didn't know existed inside me,
The poison is sweet but my hands
are far from shy,
So they reach and reach
until war rages gently in my mind,
Winning for a single fleeting second.
But keep still,
Every made-up character
that tells me this shouldn't be
will be killed by the tongue
that grazes my defence.

I will pull you inside of me
for an epic soul-searching trip,

Where this depth of passion must drown
every commitment you made without me.

My Reflection

He is my reflection in the mirror that
never shows up my imperfections.
With him, I am the most genuine image
of myself; glowing, growing and
showing the world that a woman is more
than the shadows of opinions crafted for
self-destruction.

We are the best of each other, even on
bad days when the sky gets cloudy and
the ocean tries to cover our sandy feet
with rough waves,
He keeps me anchored on shore.
Sure of the value I am to him,
Sure of the truth we live, and how I
consume every breath that God breathes
into him; so that I might live and be free!

This man is the author of every positive
book written about my life,
And the pages last a lifetime in my mind
and the words go on and on and on.

And my God! The energy is majestic,
I feel the universe shift each time he
enters my soul simply by the gentle kiss
on my tender lips.

Oh, I am free to live and to be.

He is my reflection and I am what he
sees himself to be.

We are the reflection of love that this
world refuses to let itself see.

Give Me Back Name

I am living, breathing and walking poetry.
I've already decided that any man would be
called lucky to have me.

But you gave every piece of me away,
For time chasing money that we didn't need,
Or watching our marriage bleed
gold blood over my white wedding dress.

I didn't want the love you bought in the store,
And I hated the love you forced on me as I
tried to run from this burial ground of
contaminated emotions.

When two become one, there really is no spell
or magic that can reverse it,
In fact, it should be for forever and the day
after: that is time truly spent together.

But I am living, breathing and walking poetry,
And I know you never felt lucky to have me.

So watch me go from this cemetery
just as I came.

Don't worry, John,
You can keep your last name.

Divorce

And suddenly this house is empty and
so is the place we used to call home;
It's left to be overgrown by bushes
and weeds and tall trees,
Just like our commitment,
Just like for better or worse,
Just like in sickness and health.

You once told me that no one lives to
see forever,
And you once told me you'd love
me forever,
But now I understand what forever
means while being a victim of smooth
words and a slick tongue.

Forever is not an eternity which
earthling man must achieve, nor is it
an immeasurable distance that travels
across the galaxies.
Forever is not the space we see as our
eyes close to kiss the one we love,

and it is not a feeling of bliss in the
instant of holy matrimony.

Forever is now.
Forever is the look on your face as it
spells betrayal and lies.
Forever is the moment of endless
screams bellowing through a home
made for two, crowded by infidelity,
Forever was the exact time of death
of your love for me.

Forever is the time it takes to recover
from mental abuse.
It is the kind of medication we take
for depression and the exact time it
takes to accept this new type of truth.

Shadow Defender

I don't have the best relationship with
my shadow, sometimes I feel naked
and hustle away from the awkward
gaze she offers me.
She is a dark reminder
of every bad deed I wish I could
forget and is the trophy in the room
for the battles I wish were never won.

But this shadow has a defender,
She is protected against wicked
tongues, my own ego or lies
which disturb moments of laughter.

My husband is my shadow's
defender, he stays next to her when
the world doesn't care to offer a smile,
He guards her secrets and opens
the night sky so she can shine.

My shadow has a defender,
And it makes life better on all days.

She is able to live in her element
and dance without being judged
or cry without being mocked.

My shadow has a defender who
doesn't care about her horrid past,
He holds her close to his chest
and stays when she removes the
plastic smile that is stuck on to the
mask. My shadow's defender lives
with her pain, he sleeps next to the
memories that corrupted her
childhood; he steals her sadness and
enriches her soul.

This man is the modern-day Robin
Hood. I still don't have a good
relationship with my shadow, and
that's okay.

My shadow has a defender,
So she is here to stay.

Virgin Plantation

Sex and slavery must be the same thing.

My body is captured by this stranger
and kept until my death,
Or when he is done destroying
every aspect of my being.

Wait,
Maybe sex is worse than slavery
because I have no chance of escape,
I am tied to this horrid land forever
and my body is bruised by more than
whips and chains or slaps to my face.

Sex and slavery might have a few
things in common since they both
are propagated by penises and
demons,
While one party becomes enriched
through draining the other.

Oh,
To be free, oh to be free is all I dream!
Free from the slavery of sex.

Oh, to be free is all I dream!

Please Forgive Us

Jane,
I wish you were free and
never had to worry about men
and how nasty we can be.

Jane,
Your strength inspires me
to write this story about the battles
you've won and the taste
of blood-stained victory.

Jane,
Will you forgive this world
for breaking your soul to pieces,
And are my tears just a reflection
of the ocean you cried
while being beaten,
betrayed and mistreated?

Jane,
I hope that mankind is able to see
your smile once more.

Jane,
If you cry today, it isn't the end of the
war.

Jane,
Your poetry is more than words;
it is the answer that will open doors
and free caged birds.
This stanza of your life will bring
truth
and immortality. Please, Jane,
stay with me!

Jane, please answer! Jane! Jane!

Jane,
I hope your pain is temporary
and that love is real. This darkness is
covering a light waiting to be
revealed.

Freedom from Marriage

Freedom is the sound your wedding
ring makes as it drops from your hand
onto the welcoming arms of a dirty
floor crowded by a wicked shadow.

Freedom is the feel of a violent breeze
which blows away the clutches of
abuse and power and manipulation
that once found their home around
your neck.

Ah! Yes, woman! Freedom is the
sight of your feet marching forward
into a place of peace and emotional
health. It is not on the bed that
drained your sanity and raped you of
an independence you once had and
felt.

Freedom is in the smooth movement
of the pen across the dotted line.

Every girl doesn't need to dream of a
white dress and pretty house.

My freedom is won now!
My freedom is now!

Take Me to the Garden

Never bring me flowers because it breaks my
heart to see them die. Death of anything so
beautiful should make our whole world cry.

Tell me sweet tales of the beauty in their
colours, let's sit and talk; romancing in the
fragrance while sleeping on the grass,
But please don't pick me flowers!

The time we spend in the open air never passes
as time passes. I store every word you whisper
and kiss you surrender to my sweet, sweet
soul. Happiness: we can never grow old.
Yes, bold? I am bold!

Tell me you love me! Say it again and again;
Show me you love me with simplicity,
Dance with me on the leaves; look! Butterflies
on tulips and roses growing amass.

Follow me to the end of the rainbow,
Do you hear laughter?

That's the echo of our passion now returning
as memories.

Never bring me flowers because I hate to see
them die;
If it represents your love, then never bring me
flowers to watch them die.

Take me to the garden so I can watch
your love live.

Theme: Self-Harm and Surviving Abuse

Fighting Back

Does the way my head no longer dip
to the rise and fall of your fist, make you sick?

Or are you offended by this chip on my
shoulder? It's perfectly seated as a temptation
for the next angry fighter willing to risk it all,
To touch me,
It will be the last time he touches warrior.

Life in leggings just might be a super power;
Watch me hashtag you to death, then publish
your two faces so the world could see who you
truly are, over and over and over.

Are you angered by this new tone of
confidence? Or is that the look of your face
when standing in the rays of healed and
glorious elegance?

Do you remember painting the bedroom floor
with my tears on mornings? Yes? Well, I hated
the game of Russian Roulette near the stairs

whenever I had to call on an angel to stop me
from falling.

And look at me now!
Imagine the day has come when I no longer
twitch, or crawl to a corner after tasting my
blood off your lips, because your sorry was
always accompanied by a slow and passionate kiss.
Judas!
Come kiss me again, Judas! Let me have the
pleasure of ripping out your tongue,
And hanging it for the entire world to see;
Thereby ending the songs of a changed man
that you lied and sang to me.

I'll Take the Blame

Jane, my love,
I dream to understand the pain you live,
The man that left through the back door,
Promised to fortify the front of your existence.

You should feel shallow
Living as the pleasure they can rest sure of
each cold night.
Your eyes mirror the heaviness of the soul;
One heavy soul.
That is now a mass grave,
With deposits of each partner,
And their partner,
And their partner's partner.
Jane, my love,
I don't envy the portion
society told me you chose.
Were it not for your mother,
Who was wise enough to keep
her sins a secret,
This family would've
disowned your birth and now.

You should've locked the door
and stopped dressing so sexy.
You didn't even sit with your legs closed!

You, Jane, my love,
Invited every touch.
Don't blame him
because your mother was happy.
She was wise enough to keep
their sins a secret.

Smelling the Colour Victory

My love, do you know the smell of the colour victory?
If not, let me share it with thee.
It tastes like the vibrant motion of swaying
trees that were lost in stagnation, but finally
grew the branches that would dance to the
perfect breeze.
It is the shade of confidence that now glows in
the brightest light,
It glows because light is dark when my light
shines this bright!
It smells like the taste of self-worth, which
comes bouncing off my buds; too hot to stay in
my mouth, so at every chance I sing, and I
shout: freedom! Freedom!
Freedom is the colour of victory and it smells
like the gentle ocean that knows no boundary!
Yes! This new me has the texture of the
sweetest rose that knows where to plant itself
and chooses carefully the hands that will pick
her petals. And chooses carefully the nose that
will be enchanted by her scent,
And that is the smell of the colour victory.

A fragrance that has conquered this world to
live at war with a vicious enemy,
The smell of the colour victory is the survivor
of violence seated perfect and pretty
in this dark and lonely alley,
Seated alone to smell the colour of her soon-to-be victory.

Whose Body Is This?

I feel drained. My days are spent at war with
this mirror; staring at an image that doesn't
embody the greatest reflection of the
female body.

God must have made a mistake with me.

Where are my hips? They should stand out in
this dress!
Where are my breasts? Instead, I have a solid
pain ejecting self-pity from my chest.
I can't stand the pimples in my face, they are
the reason for the barricades at my door,
I can't go out like this.

I refuse to be any less than her! Yes, her!
The one on my television screen,
Who elegantly dresses herself in the
foundation of self-esteem.
The concealer is perfectly layered over her
flaws,

This is the last straw,
I refuse to go through that door,
Alive.

Jane and Jill

Jill, keep your hands to yourself rather than
destroy a world you don't have the tools to
rebuild.

How can you sit so perfectly knowing of a life
that you helped kill?

Yes, one that you helped to kill!

Look at my feet!
Jill, please look at my feet!
Yes, they are flooded by the tears and blood
from sins you committed against me.

And while my memory of your wandering
hands is fresh, I often wonder if you took the
time or energy to put your crimes against me
to death,
Or do they linger in your mind each time we
greet each other at our annual family time.
Do your memories linger like your hands
lingered and struck a chord with invading my

body? Or are you satisfied with telling
yourself it was just girls playing, maybe?

I blame you for the confusion I felt in my mind
and body; I wasn't just a teen.

Imagine me,
Waiting to finally wake up
from that horrible dream.

Imagine me finally free from you.

Imagine you, finally, free from yourself too.

In a Man's World

Today he asked about the taste
of my cherry red lips,
And I was scarred by a firm grip
reluctantly allowed to the side
of my hip.

Yesterday was a battle to keep my clothes on
As every step I took, I missed an inch of cover
to eyes that pierced below my waistline
and just under my shoulder.

Tomorrow I'll have to remind these hunters
That I can think and that when I blink,
It's just a blink!
Not a secret code to grope me in the dark,
Nor is it an undercover sexually charged wink.

Tonight I'll travel with my purse clutched close
to my chest, hoping to hide the fact that
as a woman I have no control over the size
and beauty of my breast.

I'll practice sitting like a lady
just as the women before
who thought. My mother, my mother's mother
and me but were still raped of their identity.

But fear not my sisters,
As nightly I plot beneath the sheets
of how to emasculate this very mentality
which fights to keep us as little pure
and silent sheep.

Breathe, by nature we are born to be free!
The rib from his side has no place
under his feet.

Losing Myself

He entered my house against my will,
And since that day, I've lost every
possession a woman could truly value.

With such force he stripped the paint
from my walls, destroying any hope
of one day giving the beauty
of them to someone deserving.

And at night when my mind doesn't sleep,
I notice the most precious of
gifts that was stolen from me.

My soul;
It was snatched from between my legs,
And ripped into pieces by the same hands
that held the jewels bestowed on me at birth.

But I was brave, I looked at the bastard,
Directly in his eyes,

I wanted to show him that the fear
he searched so desperately for
had no place in this house.

I'll never fully recover from this nasty invasion,
And the flashes of when it all happened.
Like demons on steroids they haunt me daily,
And I keep looking for the eyes of the burglar
in those closest to me.

Now I live in fear of the next thief that will come,
And finish destroying the hallow house of my soul,
So I let everyone who knocks enter,
Without resistance or protest.

I Didn't Ask to Be a Slave

I didn't ask for this, and I promise you,
I wasn't dressed like the girl you say invites
this kind of horror,
I was just a little girl; a child counting time
while the monster invaded my body and
destroyed a temple of promise and purity.

And,

I promise you that I didn't ask for it.
I said no over and over and over,
But his ears were covered by the heaviness of
his ego,
An ego that claimed possession of my dress,
and then my breast, and then my truth
and finally, my freedom.

And now,

Eggshells litter every street and passageway I
traverse while searching for answers to life's
most difficult questions:

Why did you do this to me?
How did I become the victim of a war raging in your soul?
What should I do now that my innocence is yours and I feel like I don't belong in this world?
But I'll be walking,
Hoping to return one day to the moment that I was made into a slave.
Hoping to free myself;
Hoping to forgive,

Waiting to be brave.

Theme: Parental Relationships and Family Life

What Is a Father?

Do you know how to be a father?
I'm asking because I'm ready to spend
my life searching for one.

I've known breast and fluids from the day
of my birth and I'm ready to match
all I've heard to the firmness and solid
structure of this earth.

Should I look for the kindness of a kiss
on my forehead each time I shame myself?
Or do I hide from boys until he decides I am
ready to be a gift to someone else?

How does a father love his daughter?
Is it in the subtle look of disappointment
each time she fails a class? Or does it climax
with a sudden slap across the cheek when she
dares to question his proud hypocrisy?

And at night, when my mother rests with anxiety,
Should this little girl accept this as every woman's
portion in life? Will every "single" man have
several jealous wives?

Can I find a father in the lonely look in this man's eyes?
How can he be surrounded by so
much love, yet seem so distant and uneasy?
This must be what it means to be a strong and
emotionally solid daddy.
I've gone through every checkpoint in my cloudy
head, and came to the conclusion that my father
is dead.
Not to the world or in any kind of symbolic way,
But he is dead to the truth,
dead to my hurt,
Dead to the lies I've told just to get his smile or smirk.
Dead in my dreams, even the ones I have while awake.
He is dead to my desire to bring him to life.
Dead to my love, and when he goes to heaven,
I hope he notices he has passed on, because no young girl
deserves such an awful experience
of being raised by a corpse.

Hello, Stranger

Hello, stranger, it's nice to meet you.
We've exchanged smiles and shared a
common blood for so long,
But for some twisted reason, this connection
never grew strong.

Hello, stranger! Welcome to my world.
This is where I process our history and
reminisce on stories,
Reminisce on stories,
Reminisce on stories that my sister and I were
seldom told.

Hello, stranger! I think we might have a bit
more in common than you know. You've
implanted so much on me and now I get to
watch myself grow.
And yes, I grew,
From a woman who struggled with identity,
To a tower of strength
beaming light into its womb, ready for what
my own journey will be.

Hello, stranger, it's nice to meet you.
As the years crawled over, I got a glimpse at your truth.

Hello, stranger, it's me, your daughter,
And I really appreciate you!

Hello, friend,
I missed you!

Dancing with My Father

Dancing with my father was always a
challenge because of his two left feet.
Sometimes I would understand his thinking,
And sometimes it made little sense to a girl like
me.

Dancing with my father was at times a treat!
He'd make me laugh and smile, especially
when I was younger; when I was more of a
child.

The memories I have of him being an anchor
and rock are few. In fact, those memories are only the ones
others told me were true.
They say I used to cry whenever he would
leave, some say I was always hanging
jealously onto his shirt sleeve.

Dancing with my father became a burden and
sometimes a chore. He never understood the
needs of a girl who was becoming distant and
mature. So I purposefully danced around him,

hoping he would just let me be or learn to ignore.

But dancing with my father has become something I miss. I'll forget all his sins and foolish ways just for some truth and closeness.

And if I step on his feet, it will be me becoming the woman I once dreamed to be. But I hope he still dances as a demonstration of his true love and admiration for me.

A Letter to My Parents

Of all the flowers in the garden, I happen to
be the most privileged. Because through
your eyes, I see the reflection of love, self
worth and pride.

But I'm yet to gaze beyond the surface,
Or embrace the truth I lived, which to you
might be a sudden breath-taking lie.
Look at me dancing with this silver spoon,
But can't seem to tell you the moments
when my life was lost in the bliss of a new
doom.

Girls like me seldom have a fear beyond the
bogeyman man below my bed. Girls like
me hide in the closet until the bogeyman is
dead, or at least dead to me.

But you are the perfect super heroes in this
imperfect world of mine. A world I created
with distance, silence and time. And when
you rescued me, you barely knew I was in

danger; instead your thoughts were that I
found love, and I did, but with a stranger.

And when you rescued me, you were
asleep, but awake in the memories I keep of
sacrifices and dirtied hands covered over by
busted knuckles.

Oh, and when you rescued me, it was with
the evidence of pure love; the love I saw in
your eyes and in our house.

Dear Mom and Dad,
I am free!
Dear Mom and Dad,
You rescued me!

Jane and Dad

If this mirror describes what I look like,
Then I'm pleased to be my own little girl.
I've stood tall and strong,
contented to have lived life
in my beautiful and charming world.

The fact is, I've never yearned
to find someone to replace you,
And oh, how that means the most to me.
I found the strength on my own that
you didn't have to stay when every
arrow pointed for your leave.

I've met you, Dad;
In every moment I spent by alone.
I built a wall of confidence
to secure my ego with every word
this stranger said you should have said.

Just as your absence starved me
of my first innocent male touch,
I stand hungry to understand

if I'm meant to embrace my own sex
to love and honour.

Had my mother been able to describe your stature
Without becoming drained beyond her
already frail health, I would have killed her
with my curiosity after burying it so long.

Rest easy, you dead man,
I will continue to father myself
and kiss the reflection of this brave,
charming soldier in this lonely field.
To my ear, I'll whisper every beautiful
secret a girl deserves to hear.

And when I'm older,
My children will never know you
in truth or fiction,
But I'll stand in the gap and be the perfect
male reflection.

Love Letter to My Mother

I always knew that we would meet again
under the strangest of circumstances; I
planned this fatal embrace of two different
souls on an endless journey to closure.

And today when we embraced, I felt
like I was home again.
Suddenly that urge to cast you into hell
left my mind. And I was consumed
by the milk which flowed from your breast
and harnessed the energy I have now
to fight every demon that this cruel world
calls my friend.

I used to live here.
And it amazes me how you still do.
I'm touched by your new-found love
and the forgiveness left unspoken
for my father and from me to you.

These countryside sights
don't play on my tried heartstrings.
I am more familiar now with the rustle
of the town and colourful souls
that only last long enough to deceive
the innocence of the unsuspecting foreigner.

But night time falls and I have to return
to the place of my birth.
The place that birthed my creativity
and echoes the dreams of any country girl
that comes to town, regardless of the passage
and the shackles she wears.
These shackles only keep me tamed
for the world's sake.

Because if I get loose and my freedom
is finally won, I'll destroy you and
everyone who ever loved me the way
I knew was wrong.

Theme: Pregnancy and Motherhood

When Women Die

When women die, their bodies continue
to roam the earth;
Almost lifelessly at times while seeking
purpose or driven deeply into work.

My friends, simply put, when women die,
It's usually always after child birth.

Life becomes fluid through the soul
of another while dreams are surrendered
sometimes for a short time,
Or sometimes for as long as forever.

When women die, it's usually after child birth,
But it is a death they rather not trade
for all the pleasures of this earth,
So effortlessly she gives rise
to a gift to the world,
A sacred gem,
A heavenly prize,
Another vessel, another soul.

When women die, their spirits remain on earth,
And they travel through offspring
carrying treasured rituals
and wounds left uncleaned,
But when women die,
their souls can still be felt and seen.

And if this woman dies,
What will be her contribution to this place
besides the hours of drained hands
and struggle after struggle after struggle.

But if this woman dies now,
Her soul will never leave the earth;
She has immortalized herself,

She gave birth.

Ah, yes, but fear rages as an untamed storm,
So when day breaks, she releases
a gentle sigh, until night falls once more.

But if this woman dies like any other,
Her soul will remain on this earth
and travel from generation to generation,
Lifting the world out of chaos,
Calming the roughness of the oceans,
Revolutionising science and being the home
of discovery.

If this woman dies now,
This place might become poorer
because of one less body,
But when women die,
Their souls will remain on earth,
And travel through every human interaction
and live through every divine birth.

A Letter to My Daughter

I want you to be free and to explore
all the roads I never had the courage
or permission to travel.
I want you to rise with the sun
and dance with the moon,
Simply radiating in every moment
because the sky is just the beginning
of your limit.

Mommy wishes your heart to be true,
So that you'll know what real love is
or what true self love can do.

And when this world tries to steal
your God-given identity,
Mommy wants you to march forward
and launch a war against every evil force
for the sake of all humanity.

Love, big girls cry too,
And I want you to know that like an ocean,
I'll always be here waiting to engulf you

and to be the foundation on which you sail,
Or the passageway of hope when
the journey on land gets hard or fails.

Little Jane Doe,
If I'm not here when you need me,
'cause my card was called
by the card holder,
Just hold firm to every lesson
Mama has taught ya.

Oh, sweet angel of mine, I see a reflection
of something special and divine,
Your free spirit gives a mother hope
as I still battle with my own hurt.

But in your eyes, I see freedom
and life and the meaning of love.

Little Jane Doe,
I'm leaving you this letter,
So you can share it with every girl
and with every mother,
Love is selfless and it lasts forever and ever,
And when all else fails, just believe
in the pure heart of your mother,
I love you.

To Be a Mother

I have cravings late at night and early in the morning too. Sometimes when I can't sleep, I rest in bed dreaming of how I would love and care for you.

Will I experience the joys of seeing those first steps? Or must I live to wonder how mothers feel, while keeping a wound close to my chest?

I'm yet to discover the formula that qualifies anyone to be a parent. I might have to trust God until we meet, and I get to ask for the answer to that question.
But until my hour, I'll wait while hurting; I'll wait while searching. Searching for something to occupy my time…time I could've spent nursing.

My Lord, will you let me be a vessel for you? Can I feel the growth of life too?
Allow me the chance to undo the damage done

to me.
I'm forever hopeful that you'll trust me as much as
I trust you.

And if for some reason I'm rejected this
honour, just know I would have done a far
better job than my own mother.

When Cycles Don't Break

I can't wait to feel you grow inside of me,
Turning around and bringing new life,
Faith and hope to a family.

I welcome your birth with all of me,
But I'm afraid of what I'll do to you,
Simply because of what was done
To me.

A Journey of a Million Steps

I started this journey with the praise of loved
ones and friends, their energy flowed through
the atmosphere; sure of truth and happiness.

I simply did not know fear,

But as the road grew tiring, and the finish line
seemed distant with each trimester,
I was alone, I looked around and you weren't
there.

Alone with thoughts which plagued the busy
walls of my mind; curiously searching for
answers to questions that never found the ear
of my neighbour, or friend or mother.

My steps are shaky despite having travelled
this winding road before.
Sadly, my unborn daughter has me feeble,
troubled and deeply unsure.
There are no listening ears in sight; they've all
faded. Faded like memories of my favourite
childhood stories and nursery rhymes.

My steps are shaky despite having traversed this winding road before.
And the trees that were planted beside me keeping my company and offering shade, all stood covered by my shadow and will to be stronger and to be a mother,
Again.

Transforming

And when I gave birth, I lost myself
while knowing my own happiness
could no longer be first.

But who wishes first place if it means
a victory lap through life
without the bliss of unconditional love.

When nights grow silent and the world
towers with busy confusion,
My heart takes refuge in the gentle nature
of her stare and his innocent smile;
This, my friends, is the reason every mother
must have been willing to walk the extra mile.

So although our feet tremble with exhaustion
and tear drops soften the earth,
Below our already battered heels
step after step we must keep treading,
Race after race we must keep running,
And slap after slap we must keep turning,
Yes! we must keep turning cheeks

or turning keys
or turning the impossible into possibilities.

Oh, and yes, my body is tired,
But I must toil and toil and toil
because motherhood is never a human act,
But rather a complete movement of
the soul from one human being
to the other.

It is the ultimate sacrifice of life
through dying to yourself countless times
while counting time one heart beat
or heartache at a time.

So maybe someone should have told me
that I'd become a slave to the clock
and a prisoner of routines,
But they didn't.

But no one could have told me
that this is the art of always becoming
a new version of yourself
at the unintended demand of another.

No one could have prepared me
to be
mother.

Theme: Religion and Spirituality

Acceptance from Him

I have searched for you so long
without knowing I was ignorant
of what to look for.

So I lifted my voice to you
and my body carried the melody
with a rise and fall,
Step by step,
Turn after turn,
Dancing around every question
my mind wouldn't allow
my mouth to ask.

And unexpectedly you became
my perfect partner
who let me step on His toes,
But whispered forgiveness,
though I made countless steps
to the direction of an abominable end.

But when I sing now,
You are the perfect audience.
Every note for your glory,
Reminds me of an encounter with
another erasable sin.

Now that I've found you,
Or you have found me,
I think I know where my desire lives.
I'll try to put on a straight face
and walk away from soiled sheets,
crooked gazes and rainbows
that promise no gold to wonderers.

We met and danced but the world
still sees me possessed with demons.
So here I go,
Racing toward the end of this rainbow
To live a life with no colour
Just a typical family
A wife
A mother.

Walks into Heaven

Can you imagine the horror of travelling but not knowing the direction of your journey? This is the plight of every woman that seeks an encounter with the creator.
He is relentless in demands but blameless in His ways.

Oh, at night I sigh and cry and wail on these knees,
Think, for a second, of how it feels walking into heaven but never standing on your own two feet, because you were constantly told how much more of a man you needed to be.

Shall I allow hollow voices to distract me from the beauty that I see?
I'm standing erect before my God and he is happy with me.

I'm broken because someone touched me too soon and
I feel trapped in a body that is not my own.

I lived for so many people besides myself
that now that I'm dead,
I'm not sure what this should feel like.

So kiss me sweet Master, and allow your fire
to cleanse my doubt!
This is our time now;
Let me sit at your feet and learn
the truth about You.

Living in My Garden

There was no special care of any kind,
Or tender hands that clipped thorns,
Which grew wild and unnoticed
by a mother's gaze.

I've given up on growing like hibiscus,
Which smells so sweet at the morning's kiss,
And certainly, tulips have no place here.

This is a place where weeds wrestle
with ambition;
They leave nothing but straggled stems,
And fallen petals that tell
tales only to the dirt.
Who picks up dead petals
to inhale the true value of a rose?

This soil will never grow orchids,
But I envy every type of beauty,
Stretching from the core
of my neighbour's bed.

Maybe I'll stand in the hot, hot sun,
And allow every ray to dissect
the loneliness, rape and tears.
And when the rains come,
It better wash away every desire
I've had to live in your shadow,
So the world can watch me grow.

And I hope my gardener will
pick me from this polluted world,
And spare no effort of the weeds
returning the favour,
And let you taste the dirt
I sprung through.

Insecurities
(Featured Poet)

If only our insecurities didn't control us.
Would we be able to see the wonder and beauty of the world sitting right before us?
If only our insecurities didn't drown us.
Would we take that deep breath, push our heads out the water and ride the tide to the shores of greatness
waiting patiently around us?
If only our insecurities didn't hide us.
Would the cloudy mirror that we view ourselves through be forced to remove its soot and rust, bind broken
glass and disperse the dust, to reflect so clearly the very beauty within us?
If only our insecurities didn't bind us.
Would we rise from the corner, push past the crowd of naysayers and see the path pieced together so clearly
by our Creator, waiting for us to walk proudly, head held high, demanding the respect and self-worth deserved
by us?
If only our insecurities didn't shut us up.
Would we speak openly, address our failures, our fears, our brokenness, our tears,

The emptiness juxtaposing the fullness that sits deep within us.
If only our insecurities didn't define us.
We'd see ourselves for who we are, sit comfortably in our truth and never fear to reach out and share.
Me with you!
Building and pushing each other each other,
Cancelling the negative, propelling the positive and existing in a world that really reacted the very meaning of
life within us.
If only our insecurities would
Inspire…Us
Nurture…Us
Support…Us
Enrich…Us
Celebrate…Us
Uplift…Us
Reimage…Us
Illuminate…Us
Transform…Us
Invigorate…Us
Encourage…Us
Steady…Us
Then we'd more readily be able to genuinely LOVE us.

Jaleesa Daniel
05.06.18

The Cover Poem
Being Jane Doe

Being Jane Doe is no task for a man
Because they seldom live through rejection
and can't bear pain without stretching
out to every passing hand.
Wearing leggings is no job for a guy,
For time after time they will die
from piercing eyes and uninvited touches.

Being Jane Doe is more than being a woman;
It is becoming life when death feels sure,
Or popular and simply common,
It is the art of living through self-pity
and pride.
Being Jane Doe is learning how to keep
secrets until comfort pierces the soul from
someone outside.

Ah, our feet get weak and sometimes
our hearts grow tired. And in the midst of darkness,
We must find strength to slay dragons and cast spells on
demons,

All while being Jane Doe and a mother
And a sister and a wife.
Oh, look on the counter sits an attractive knife,
But I have no time to think of killing myself,
At least not before making dinner or cleaning the house
while acting as father.

Being Jane Doe is no task for a man!

Unless this man understands that we aren't from the same places,
Or blessed with the same graces and will never share
the same spaces until he stands up when they tell us to sit and shut-up
or to move over while sliding hands invade our crutch.

Jane Doe has to be a woman who
eventually frees herself from cages,
She must be the type of woman that demands
equal treatment and equal wages.
It isn't good enough for her to sit silently on our chest,
Jane Doe is a woman and women are eternal at best,
And at her worse, Jane Doe still manages to shine through hell
and warm the hearts of those who hurt.

This is why Jane Doe can't be a man;
Their stories aren't the same and this
he will never understand.

There is one hope that might save mankind,
But they must be willing to listen,

And then write her through poetry as
new life lessons.

Jane Doe is a woman in every woman,
And she has a story to be told,
So look into her eyes and read the pages
of her soul.

Jane Doe is a woman designed, inspired
and ordained to change this world.

END

CPSIA information can be obtained
at www.ICGtesting.com
Printed in the USA
BVHW070010151221
624011BV00023B/1951